CONTENTS

Tunes included in VOLUME 123 are:

MW00565321

Any codas (⊕) that appear will be played only once
on the recording at the end of the <u>last</u> recorded chorus.

PLAY-A-LONG CD INFORMATION
STEREO SEPARATION: LEFT CHANNEL=Organ, Bass & Drums; RIGHT CHANNEL=Guitar & Drums
TUNING NOTES: Concert Bb & A (A=440) • CD RECORDED at THE JAZZ FACTORY, Louisville, KY
PERSONNEL ON PLAY-A-LONG RECORDING
JOEY DEFRANCESCO - Organ; PAUL BOLLENBACK - Guitar; BYRON LANDHAM - Drums

Published by
JAMEY AEBERSOLD JAZZ®
P.O. Box 1244
New Albany, IN 47151-1244
www.jazzbooks.com
ISBN 978-1-56224-162-9

Cover Design
PATRICK McLAUGHLIN

Cover Photo
At THE JAZZ FACTORY
JAMEY AEBERSOLD

Engraving
DAVID SILBERMAN

Layout
JASON A. LINDSEY

BOOK ONLY: $5.95 U.S.

NOTES TO THE MUSICIAN

There was a time when I didn't particularly enjoy jazz organ trios. In my teenage years, the organ was what I heard in my Methodist church so I associated the instrument with hymns, people singing and church.

As jazz evolved and Jimmy Smith and Larry Young entered my jazz record library I learned to love the sound of the Hammond B3 in a jazz setting. I grew up near Louisville, Kentucky and after receiving my driver's license, I would frequent night clubs where often there was an organ trio or quartet playing. On nights when I really felt brave, I would ask to sit in and play a song or two with them. This was part of my early musical bandstand training and it was very important to me.

This Volume 123 Play-A-Long has an outstanding organ trio led by Joey DeFrancesco. Joey, Paul and Byron are Joey's original trio and have played on and off together for many years. I was fortunate to record them on February 14, 2008 at The Jazz Factory in Louisville, Ky., just six weeks before the Jazz Factory closed its doors for good. The trio had played there the night before to a packed house.

Some of the songs on this set are on other sets but not in the organ trio format. Usually, when we duplicate a song, we change the tempo or key, or instrumentation and this always gives the rendition a completely different feel.

The set opens with *"Now's the Time, "* written by Charlie Parker and has become a standard blues that is probably the most called jam blues of all time. *"Four on Six"* by Wes Montgomery, is a contrafact written on the chords to *Summertime*. A contrafact is a new melody written over existing chords. The chords that Wes uses have a lot of ii/V7 substitutes and present a melodic challenge to say the least. *"The More I See You"* is an old standard with a nice harmonic flow and simple melody. *"Mercy, Mercy, Mercy"* by Joe Zawinul is his most famous song and has been played and arranged many different ways over the years. The solo section is on two chords which makes it approachable by beginning level jazzers. *"Lunch Portion"* is an original I wrote for Joey's trio. It's a shuffle and at first, makes you think it's going to be a 12 bar blues but it's not. The last two bars of each chorus take you up to the clouds. One of the prettiest ballads ever written is *"I Fall In Love Too Easily."* It's a master piece in 16 measures and is taken at a very slow tempo. The old jazz standard *"Bye, Bye, Blackbird"* shows off the trio's ability to set a groove and keep it. After the first chorus, we substitute some descending ii/ V7's over the bridge section to add variety. *"Gee Baby, Ain't I Good To You"* is a sixteen bar tune with several unusual harmonic twists here and there. It's done very slowly and reminds me of the days when I would go hear organ trios grinding out late night jazz in Louisville or Indianapolis. We decided to do *"Indiana"* even though it's on other Play-A-Long sets. Someone on our jazz forum suggested doing it at a slower tempo so that's what we did. The coda section goes to a Bossa nova feel. The *"February 14th"* title comes from the day we recorded this set. It has a great little shuffle feel with a bridge that seems to float up to the sky. *"Anthropology"* is another tune written by Charlie Parker and is based on rhythm changes. The melody is very notey and is a demonstration of the technical facility "Bird" had on his alto saxophone. *"Summertime"* is by George Gershwin and may be the most popular American standard ever. For variety, we moved this version to the key of C minor and did it at a slow tempo. *"I'm Getting Sentimental Over You"* has always been a tune jazz musicians loved to play on. The chords move around just enough to keep you on your toes. *"Slow Blues"* is just that ... a very slow blues in G. Need more be said? This CD was recorded while the famous Democratic Presidential primary was taking place in America between Hillary Clinton and Barack Obama. *"Obama-Nation"* is a take off on something I saw in the local newspaper's "letters to the editor" section during that time. The writer said, "If Obama gets elected President it will be an Obamanation." I think they said it in jest.

If you like playing jazz, this set will give you hours of enjoyable opportunities and enhance your musical skills along the way.

Jamey Aebersold -- June 2008

NOMENCLATURE

LEGEND: + or ♯ = raise 1/2 step; — or ♭ = lower 1/2 step; H = Half Step; W = Whole Step

Because jazz players, composers, educators and authors haven't agreed on a common nomenclature for writing chord and scale symbols, the novice will have to become familiar with several different ways of writing the same scale sound.

Listed below are the most common symbols in order of usage - most-used to least-used. The symbol that is boldface is the one I use most often. Notice that throughout this book you will see CΔ and C to designate a major chord/scale sound. I am doing this so you can begin to get better acquainted with various nomenclature.

Δ = Major scale/chord or major seventh (CΔ). A (7) after a letter means to lower the 7th note of the scale, making it a Dominant 7th quality (C7). A dash (—) when located beside a letter means to lower the third and seventh of the scale 1/2 step, thus making it a minor tonality (Dorian minor) (C—). Ø means half-diminished (CØ). C—Δ means a minor scale/chord with a major 7th. —3 means 3 half-steps (a minor 3rd). A ° beside a letter means diminished (C° = diminished scale/chord).

CHORD/SCALE TYPE	ABBREVIATED CHORD/SCALE SYMBOL	
✱ MAJOR (Ionian) (WWHWWWH) C D E F G A B C	**C CΔ**	Cmaj, Cma, Cma7, Cmaj7, CM, CM7, Cmaj9, Cmaj13
✱ DOMINANT SEVENTH (Mixolydian) (WWHWWHW) 5th Mode of Major: C D E F G A B♭ C	**C7**	C9, C11, C13
✱ MINOR SEVENTH (Dorian) (WHWWWHW) 2nd Mode of Major: C D E♭ F G A B♭ C	**C— C-7**	Cmi, Cmi7, Cm7, Cmin, Cmin7, Cm9, Cm11, Cm13
LYDIAN (Major Scale with ♯4) (WWWHWWH) 4th Mode of Major: C D E F♯ G A B C	**CΔ+4**	Cmaj+4, CM+4, CΔ+11, CΔ♭5, Cmaj♭5
✱ HALF-DIMINISHED (Locrian) (HWWHWWW) 7th Mode of Major: C D♭ E♭ F G♭ A♭ B♭ C	**CØ**	Cmi7(♭5), C-7♭5
HALF-DIMINISHED #2 (Locrian #2) (WHWHWWW) 6th Mode of Melodic Minor: C D E♭ F G♭ A♭ B♭ C	**CØ♯2**	CØ+2, CØ9
DIMINISHED (WHWHWHWH) C D E♭ F G♭ A♭ A B C	**C°**	Cdim, C°7, Cdim7, C°9
LYDIAN DOMINANT (Dom. 7th with ♯4) (WWWHWHW) 4th Mode of Melodic Minor: C D E F♯ G A B♭ C	**C7+4**	C7+11, C7♭5, C9+11, C13+11
WHOLE-TONE (WWWWWW) C D E F# G# Bb C	**C7+**	+4 C7aug, C7+5, C7+5
DOMINANT SEVENTH (Using a Dim. Scale) (HWHWHWHW) C D♭ E♭ E F♯ G A B♭ C	**C7♭9**	+9 +9 C7♭9+4, C13♭9+11
DIMINISHED WHOLE-TONE (Altered Scale) (HWWWWWW) 7th Mode of Melodic Minor: C D♭ E♭ E F♯ G♯ B♭ C	**C7+9**	+9+5 +9♭13 C7alt, C7♭9+4, C7♭9+11
LYDIAN AUGMENTED (Major with ♯4 & ♯5) (WWWWHWH) 3rd Mode of Melodic Minor: C D E F♯ G♯ A B C	**CΔ+4** +5	CΔ+5
MELODIC MINOR (Ascending Only) (WHWWWWH) C D E♭ F G A B C	**C—Δ**	Cmin(maj7), CmiΔ, C—Δ (Melodic), Cm6
HARMONIC MINOR (WHWWH—3H) C D E♭ F G A♭ B C	**C—Δ**	CmiΔ, C—Δ (Har), C—Δ♭6
SUSPENDED 4th (W—3WWHW) or (WWHWWHW) C D F G A B♭ C or C D E F G A B♭ C	**G—** **C**	G-7, C7sus4, C7sus, C4, C11 C
✱ BLUES SCALE (Use at player's discretion) (—3WHH—3W) (1, ♭3, 4, ♯4, 5, ♭7, 1) C E♭ F F♯ G B♭ C	(There is no chord symbol for the Blues Scale) Used mostly with dominant and minor chords)	

✱ These are the most common chord/scales in Western Music.

I believe in a reduced chord/scale notation that allows our creative side, our natural side (right brain function) to have direction and guidance without feeling inhibited or limited. **When we speak of "quality" we mean whether it is Major, Minor, Dim., or whatever.** I have tried to standardize the chord/scale symbol notation in my books. Since some have been out many years there are instances where I may have used a different chord symbol in one book than I used in this one.

I feel the improvisor needs as little notation as possible in order to transcend the actual nomenclature on the page. The more numbers, letters and alterations that appear on the page, the less chance they will have to remove their thoughts from the written page and express what is being heard in their mind. That is why I prefer **C, C7, C—, CØ, C7+9, C7♭9.** Remember, we are playing a music called jazz, and it contains many altered tones. Once we learn the various alterations and their corresponding abbreviated chord symbol, why keep writing all the alterations beside the chord symbol? Check out carefully the Scale Syllabus! Listen to Volume 26 "The Scale Syllabus."

Remember: 2nd's are the same as 9th's, 4th's are the same as 11th's, 13th's are the same as 6th's. Example: Key of C ... the 2nd, D, is the same as the 9th, D. Often a composer will simply write their preferred name of the scale beside the chord symbol, such as E♭—Δ (melodic minor), F— (phrygian), F— (phry).

Concert Key Instruments Chord Progressions
1. Now's The Time

PLAY 14 CHORUSES (♩ = 120)

Charlie Parker

(1st time only)

SOLOS

CODA

2. Four On Six

John L. (Wes) Montgomery

PLAY 15 CHORUSES (♩ = 224)

Copyright © 1960, renewed 1988 TAGGIE MUSIC CO., a division of Gopam Enterprises, Inc.
All Rights Reserved   International Copyright Secured   Used By Permission

2

3. The More I See You
(from "Diamond Horseshoe")

PLAY 5 CHORUSES (♩ = 100)

Music by Harry Warren
Lyrics by Mack Gordon

3. The More I See You – Cont.

SOLOS

| E♭Δ | A♭7 | G –7 | C7 | F –7 | | B♭7 | |

| E♭Δ | A♭7 | G –7 | C7 | F –7 | | B♭7 | |

Bridge

| E♭–7 | | D♭–7 | G♭7 | BΔ | | B♭7+9 | |

| E♭–7 | | C –7 | F7 | F –7/B♭ | | | ⁒ |

| E♭Δ | F –7 | G –7 | C7 | F –7 | | B♭7 | |

| E♭Δ | F –7 | G –7 | C7 | B♭–7 | | E♭7 | |

| A♭Δ | | D♭7 | | G –7 | | A♭–7 | D♭7 |

| G –7 | C7 | F –7 | B♭7 | ⊕ E♭Δ | | F –7 | B♭7 |

⊕ **CODA**

| GØ | | C7+9 | | AØ | A♭–7 | G –7 | F♯–7 | F –7 | EΔ | E♭Δ+4 ⌢ |

4. Mercy, Mercy, Mercy

Josef Zawinul

5

5. Lunch Portion

Jamey Aebersold

6. I Fall In Love Too Easily

Music by Jule Styne
Lyrics by Sammy Cahn

PLAY 4 CHORUSES (♩ = 54)

7

7. Bye Bye Blackbird

Words by Mort Dixon
Music by Ray Henderson

8. Gee Baby, Ain't I Good To You

PLAY 5 CHORUSES (♩ = 66)

Music by Don Redman
Lyrics by Don Redman and Andy Razaf

9. Indiana
(Back Home Again In Indiana)

PLAY 5 CHORUSES (♩ = 132)

Words by Ballard MacDonald
Music by James F. Hanley

10. February 14th

Jamey Aebersold

11

11. Anthropology

By Charlie Parker

12. Summertime
(from "Porgy and Bess")

PLAY 8 CHORUSES (♩ = 108)

Music and Lyrics by George Gershwin,
DuBose and Dorothy Heyward and Ira Gershwin

13. I'm Getting Sentimental Over You

Words by Ned Washington
Music by George Bassman

PLAY 5 CHORUSES (♩ = 144)

14

14. Slow Blues

PLAY 5 CHORUSES (♩ = 60)

Jamey Aebersold

15. Obama-Nation

Jamey Aebersold

PLAY 5 CHORUSES (♩ = 124)

Bb Instruments Chord Progressions
1. Now's The Time

PLAY 14 CHORUSES ($\bullet$ = 120)

Charlie Parker

SOLOS

CODA

17

2. Four On Six

John L. (Wes) Montgomery

PLAY 15 CHORUSES ($\bullet$ = 224)

18

3. The More I See You

(from "Diamond Horseshoe")

Music by Harry Warren
Lyrics by Mack Gordon

PLAY 5 CHORUSES (♩ = 100)

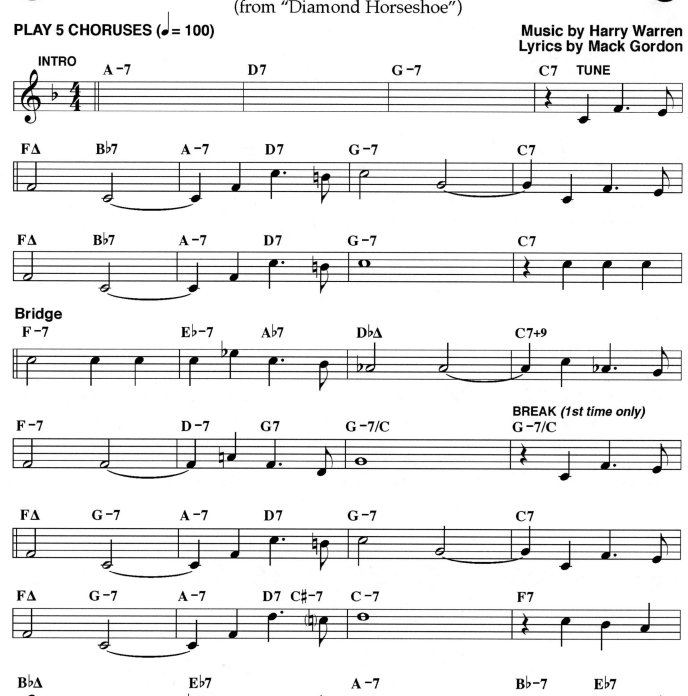

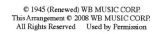

3. The More I See You – Cont.

SOLOS

| FΔ | B♭7 | A–7 | D7 | G–7 | | C7 | |

| FΔ | B♭7 | A–7 | D7 | G–7 | | C7 | |

Bridge

| F–7 | | E♭–7 | A♭7 | D♭Δ | | C7+9 | |

| F–7 | | D–7 | G7 | G–7/C | | ℅ | |

| FΔ | G–7 | A–7 | D7 | G–7 | | C7 | |

| FΔ | G–7 | A–7 | D7 | C–7 | | F7 | |

| B♭Δ | | E♭7 | | A–7 | | B♭–7 | E♭7 |

| A–7 | D7 | G–7 | C7 | 𝄋 FΔ | | G–7 | C7 |

𝄋 CODA

| AØ | | D7+9 | | BØ | B♭–7 | A–7 A♭–7 | G–7 | G♭Δ | FΔ+4 |

20

4. Mercy, Mercy, Mercy

Josef Zawinul

21

5. Lunch Portion

6. I Fall In Love Too Easily

PLAY 4 CHORUSES (♩ = 54)

Music by Jule Styne
Lyrics by Sammy Cahn

Words by Mort Dixon
Music by Ray Henderson

PLAY 6 CHORUSES (♩ = 150)

8. Gee Baby, Ain't I Good To You

PLAY 5 CHORUSES (♩ = 66)

Music by Don Redman
Lyrics by Don Redman and Andy Razaf

25

9. Indiana
(Back Home Again In Indiana)

PLAY 5 CHORUSES (♩ = 132)

Words by Ballard MacDonald
Music by James F. Hanley

10. February 14th

Jamey Aebersold

Fine

11. Anthropology

By Charlie Parker

28

12. Summertime
(from "Porgy and Bess")

PLAY 8 CHORUSES (♩ = 108)

**Music and Lyrics by George Gershwin,
DuBose and Dorothy Heyward and Ira Gershwin**

29

13. I'm Getting Sentimental Over You

Words by Ned Washington
Music by George Bassman

PLAY 5 CHORUSES (♩ = 144)

14. Slow Blues

PLAY 5 CHORUSES (♩ = 60)

Jamey Aebersold

31

15. Obama-Nation

PLAY 5 CHORUSES (♩ = 124)

Jamey Aebersold

Eb Instruments Chord Progressions
1. Now's The Time

PLAY 14 CHORUSES (♩ = 120)

Charlie Parker

(1st time only)

SOLOS

CODA

2. Four On Six

John L. (Wes) Montgomery

3. The More I See You
(from "Diamond Horseshoe")

PLAY 5 CHORUSES (♩ = 100)

**Music by Harry Warren
Lyrics by Mack Gordon**

35

SOLOS

CΔ	F7	E–7	A7	D–7		G7

CΔ	F7	E–7	A7	D–7		G7

Bridge

C–7		Bb–7	Eb7	AbΔ		G7+9

C–7		A–7	D7	D–7/G		℅

CΔ	D–7	E–7	A7	D–7		G7

CΔ	D–7	E–7	A7	G–7		C7

FΔ		Bb7	E–7	F–7	Bb7

E–7	A7	D–7	G7	⊕ CΔ		D–7	G7

⊕ **CODA**

EØ	A7+9	F♯Ø	F–7	E–7 Eb–7	D–7 DbΔ	CΔ+4

4. Mercy, Mercy, Mercy

Josef Zawinul

37

5. Lunch Portion

PLAY 11 CHORUSES (♩ = 130)

Jamey Aebersold

6. I Fall In Love Too Easily

PLAY 4 CHORUSES (♩ = 54)

Music by Jule Styne
Lyrics by Sammy Cahn

7. Bye Bye Blackbird

Words by Mort Dixon
Music by Ray Henderson

8. Gee Baby, Ain't I Good To You

PLAY 5 CHORUSES (♩ = 66)

Music by Don Redman
Lyrics by Don Redman and Andy Razaf

9. Indiana
(Back Home Again In Indiana)

Words by Ballard MacDonald
Music by James F. Hanley

PLAY 5 CHORUSES (♩ = 132)

10. February 14th

Jamey Aebersold

PLAY 4 CHORUSES (♩ = 124)

11. Anthropology

By Charlie Parker

PLAY 7 CHORUSES (♩ = 194)

12. Summertime

(from "Porgy and Bess")

Music and Lyrics by George Gershwin, DuBose and Dorothy Heyward and Ira Gershwin

13. I'm Getting Sentimental Over You

Words by Ned Washington
Music by George Bassman

14. Slow Blues

PLAY 5 CHORUSES (♩ = 60)

Jamey Aebersold

15. Obama-Nation

PLAY 5 CHORUSES (♩ = 124)

Jamey Aebersold

Bass Clef Instruments Chord Progressions
1. Now's The Time

PLAY 14 CHORUSES (♩ = 120)

Charlie Parker

2. Four On Six

PLAY 15 CHORUSES (♩ = 224)

John L. (Wes) Montgomery

3. The More I See You
(from "Diamond Horseshoe")

PLAY 5 CHORUSES (♩ = 100)

Music by Harry Warren
Lyrics by Mack Gordon

51

SOLOS

Eb△	Ab7	G–7	C7	F–7		Bb7

Eb△	Ab7	G–7	C7	F–7		Bb7

Bridge

Eb–7		Db–7	Gb7	B△		Bb7+9

Eb–7		C–7	F7	F–7/Bb		℅

Eb△	F–7	G–7	C7	F–7		Bb7

Eb△	F–7	G–7	C7	Bb–7		Eb7

Ab△		Db7		G–7		Ab–7	Db7

G–7	C7	F–7	Bb7	⊕ Eb△		F–7	Bb7

⊕ CODA

GØ		C7+9		AØ	Ab–7	G–7	F#–7	F–7	E△	Eb△+4

52

4. Mercy, Mercy, Mercy

Josef Zawinul

5. Lunch Portion

6. I Fall In Love Too Easily

PLAY 4 CHORUSES (♩ = 54)

Music by Jule Styne
Lyrics by Sammy Cahn

7. Bye Bye Blackbird

Words by Mort Dixon
Music by Ray Henderson

PLAY 6 CHORUSES (♩ = 150)

8. Gee Baby, Ain't I Good To You

PLAY 5 CHORUSES (♩ = 66)

Music by Don Redman
Lyrics by Don Redman and Andy Razaf

9. Indiana
(Back Home Again In Indiana)

PLAY 5 CHORUSES (♩ = 132)

Words by Ballard MacDonald
Music by James F. Hanley

10. February 14th

Jamey Aebersold

11. Anthropology

By Charlie Parker

60

12. Summertime

(from "Porgy and Bess")

Music and Lyrics by George Gershwin, DuBose and Dorothy Heyward and Ira Gershwin

PLAY 8 CHORUSES (♩ = 108)

13. I'm Getting Sentimental Over You

Words by Ned Washington
Music by George Bassman

14. Slow Blues

Jamey Aebersold

PLAY 5 CHORUSES (♩ = 60)

SOLOS

CODA

ritard.

15. Obama-Nation

PLAY 5 CHORUSES (♩ = 124)

Jamey Aebersold

JAMEY AEBERSOLD JAZZ® PLAY-A-LONGS

Each Play-A-Long contains at least one stereo CD and a coordinated booklet with parts FOR ALL INSTRUMENTS. The volumes do not necessarily get progressively more difficult. Popularly termed *"The Most Widely-Used Improvisation Tools On The Market!"*

The special stereo separation technique is ideal for use by rhythm players.
The left channel includes bass and drums, while the right channel contains piano or guitar and drums.

"Anyone Can Improvise" by Jamey Aebersold
BEST-SELLING DVD ON JAZZ IMPROV!
2-HOUR DVD Featuring Jamey only $19.95

JAMEY'S SUGGESTED ORDER OF STUDY: Volumes 1, 24, 21, 116, 2, 54, 3, 70, 5, 84, etc. **Vol. 1 and 24 work to form a strong foundation.**

☑	VOL.#	TITLE	FORMAT	PRICE		☑	VOL.#	TITLE	FORMAT	PRICE
❏	1	"JAZZ: HOW TO PLAY AND IMPROVISE"	BK/CD	15.90		❏	67	"TUNE UP"	BK/CD	9.95
❏	2	"NOTHIN' BUT BLUES"	BK/CD	15.90		❏	68	"GIANT STEPS"	BK/CD	15.90
❏	3	"THE II/V7/I PROGRESSION"	BK/2CDs	19.95		❏	69	CHARLIE PARKER - "BIRD GOES LATIN"	BK/CD	15.90
❏	4	"MOVIN' ON"	BK/CD	14.90		❏	70	"KILLER JOE"	BK/CD	15.90
❏	5	"TIME TO PLAY MUSIC"	BK/CD	15.90		❏	71	"EAST OF THE SUN"	BK/CD	15.90
❏	6	CHARLIE PARKER - "ALL BIRD"	BK/CD	15.90		❏	72	"STREET OF DREAMS"	BK/CD	15.90
❏	7	MILES DAVIS	BK/CD	14.90		❏	73	OLIVER NELSON - "STOLEN MOMENTS"	BK/CD	15.90
❏	8	SONNY ROLLINS	BK/CD	15.90		❏	74	"LATIN JAZZ"	BK/CD	15.90
❏	9	WOODY SHAW	BK/CD	15.90		❏	75	"COUNTDOWN TO GIANT STEPS"	BK/2CDs	19.95
❏	10	DAVID BAKER - "EIGHT CLASSIC JAZZ ORIGINALS"	BK/CD	9.95		❏	76	DAVID BAKER - "HOW TO LEARN TUNES"	BK/2CDs	19.95
❏	11	HERBIE HANCOCK	BK/CD	15.90		❏	77	PAQUITO D'RIVERA	BK/CD	15.90
❏	12	DUKE ELLINGTON	BK/CD	15.90		❏	78	"JAZZ HOLIDAY CLASSICS"	BK/CD	15.90
❏	13	CANNONBALL ADDERLEY	BK/CD	15.90		❏	79	"AVALON"	BK/CD	9.95
❏	14	BENNY GOLSON - "EIGHT JAZZ CLASSICS"	BK/CD	15.90		❏	80	"INDIANA"	BK/CD	9.95
❏	15	"PAYIN' DUES"	BK/CD	15.90		❏	81	DAVID LIEBMAN - "STANDARDS & ORIGINALS"	BK/CD	9.95
❏	16	"TURNAROUNDS, CYCLES, & II/V7s"	BK/4CDs	19.95		❏	82	DEXTER GORDON	BK/CD	15.90
❏	17	HORACE SLIVER	BK/CD	15.90		❏	83	THE BRECKER BROTHERS	BK/CD	16.90
❏	18	HORACE SILVER	BK/CD	15.90		❏	84	DOMINANT 7TH WORKOUT	BK/2CDs	19.95
❏	19	DAVID LIEBMAN	BK/CD	15.90		❏	85	ANDY LAVERNE-"TUNES YOU THOUGHT YOU KNEW"	BK/CD	15.90
❏	20	JIMMY RANEY w/GUITAR	BK/CD	15.90		❏	86	HORACE SILVER - "SHOUTIN' OUT"	BK/CD	9.95
❏	21	"GETTIN' IT TOGETHER"	BK/2CDs	19.95		❏	87	BENNY CARTER - "WHEN LIGHTS ARE LOW"	BK/CD	9.95
❏	22	"FAVORITE STANDARDS"	BK/2CDs	19.95		❏	88	"MILLENNIUM BLUES"	BK/CD	9.95
❏	23	"ONE DOZEN STANDARDS"	BK/2CDs	19.95		❏	89	"DARN THAT DREAM"	BK/CD	15.90
❏	24	"MAJOR & MINOR"	BK/2CDs	19.95		❏	90	"ODD TIMES"	BK/CD	15.90
❏	25	"ALL-TIME STANDARDS"	BK/2CDs	19.95		❏	91	"PLAYER'S CHOICE"	BK/CD	9.95
❏	26	"THE SCALE SYLLABUS"	BK/2CDs	15.00		❏	92	LENNIE NIEHAUS	BK/CD	9.95
❏	27	JOHN COLTRANE	BK/CD	15.90		❏	93	"WHAT'S NEW?"	BK/CD	15.90
❏	28	JOHN COLTRANE	BK/CD	15.90		❏	94	"HOT HOUSE"	BK/CD	9.95
❏	29	"PLAY DUETS WITH JIMMY RANEY" w/GUITAR	BK/CD	14.90		❏	95	"500 MILES HIGH"	BK/CD	15.90
❏	30A	"RHYTHM SECTION WORKOUT" - PIANO & GUITAR	BK/CD	14.90		❏	96	DAVE SAMUELS - "LATIN QUARTER"	BK/CD	15.90
❏	30B	"RHYTHM SECTION WORKOUT" - BASS & DRUMS	BK/CD	14.90		❏	97	"STANDARDS WITH STRINGS"	BK/CD	16.90
❏	31	"JAZZ BOSSA NOVAS"	BK/CD	15.90		❏	98	ANTONIO CARLOS JOBIM w/GUITAR	BK/CD	15.90
❏	32	"BALLADS"	BK/CD	15.90		❏	99	TADD DAMERON - "SOULTRANE"	BK/CD	15.90
❏	33	WAYNE SHORTER	BK/2CDs	19.95		❏	100	"ST LOUIS BLUES" DIXIELAND	BK/CD	15.90
❏	34	"JAM SESSION"	BK/2CDs	19.95		❏	101	ANDY LAVERNE - "SECRET OF THE ANDES"	BK/CD	15.90
❏	35	CEDAR WALTON	BK/CD	14.90		❏	102	JERRY BERGONZI - "SOUND ADVICE"	BK/CD	9.95
❏	36	"BEBOP AND BEYOND"	BK/CD	14.90		❏	103	DAVID SANBORN	BK/CD	16.90
❏	37	SAMMY NESTICO	BK/CD	9.95		❏	104	KENNY WERNER - "FREE PLAY"	BK/CD	15.90
❏	38	"CLASSIC SONGS FROM THE BLUE NOTE JAZZ ERA"	BK/2CDs	19.95		❏	105	DAVE BRUBECK - "IN YOUR OWN SWEET WAY"	BK/CD	15.90
❏	39	"SWING, SWING, SWING"	BK/CD	15.90		❏	106	LEE MORGAN - "SIDEWINDER"	BK/CD	15.90
❏	40	"'ROUND MIDNIGHT"	BK/2CDs	19.95		❏	107	"IT HAD TO BE YOU!" - STANDARDS FOR SINGERS	BK/2CDs	19.95
❏	41	"BODY AND SOUL"	BK/2CDs	19.95		❏	108	JOE HENDERSON - "INNER URGE"	BK/CD	15.90
❏	42	"BLUES IN ALL KEYS"	BK/CD	15.90		❏	109	DAN HAERLE - "FUSION"	BK/CD	15.90
❏	43	"GROOVIN' HIGH"	BK/CD	15.90		❏	110	"WHEN I FALL IN LOVE" - ROMANTIC BALLADS	BK/CD	15.90
❏	44	"AUTUMN LEAVES"	BK/CD	15.90		❏	111	JJ JOHNSON	BK/CD	15.90
❏	45	BILL EVANS	BK/CD	15.90		❏	112	COLE PORTER - "21 GREAT STANDARDS"	BK/2CDs	19.95
❏	46	"OUT OF THIS WORLD"	BK/CD	15.90		❏	113	"EMBRACEABLE YOU" - BALLADS FOR ALL SINGERS	BK/2CDs	19.95
❏	47	"I GOT RHYTHM CHANGES" - IN ALL KEYS	BK/CD	15.90		❏	114	"GOOD TIME"	BK/4CDs	19.95
❏	48	DUKE ELLINGTON - "IN A MELLOW TONE"	BK/CD	15.90		❏	115	RON CARTER	BK/2CDs	16.90
❏	49	"SUGAR" w/ORGAN	BK/CD	14.90		❏	116	"MILES OF MODES" - MODAL JAZZ	BK/2CDs	19.95
❏	50	MILES DAVIS - "THE MAGIC OF MILES"	BK/CD	15.90		❏	117	"COLE PORTER FOR SINGERS"	BK/2CDs	19.95
❏	51	"NIGHT & DAY"	BK/CD	15.90		❏	118	JOEY DEFRANCESCO - "GROOVIN' JAZZ" w/ORGAN	BK/CD	15.90
❏	52	"COLLECTOR'S ITEMS"	BK/CD	15.90		❏	119	BOBBY WATSON	BK/CD	9.95
❏	54	"MAIDEN VOYAGE"	BK/CD.	15.90		❏	120	"FEELIN' GOOD" - BLUES IN B-3 w/ORGAN	BK/CD	15.90
❏	55	JEROME KERN - "YESTERDAYS"	BK/CD	14.90		❏	121	PHIL WOODS	BK/CD	15.90
❏	56	THELONIOUS MONK	BK/CD	15.90		❏	122	JIMMY HEATH	BK/CD	15.90
❏	57	"MINOR BLUES IN ALL KEYS"	BK/CD	15.90		❏	123	"NOW'S THE TIME" - JOEY DEFRANCESCO TRIO w/ORGAN	BK/CD	15.90
❏	58	"UNFORGETTABLE STANDARDS"	BK/CD	14.90		❏	124	"BRAZILIAN JAZZ"	BK/CD	15.90
❏	59	"INVITATION" w/ORGAN	BK/2CDs	19.95		❏	125	"CHRISTMAS CAROL CLASSICS"	BK/CD	16.90
❏	60	FREDDIE HUBBARD	BK/CD	15.90		❏	126	RANDY BRECKER w/RANDY BRECKER	BK/2CDs	19.95
❏	61	"BURNIN'"	BK/CD	15.90		❏	127	EDDIE HARRIS - "LISTEN HERE"	BK/CD	15.90
❏	62	WES MONTGOMERY	BK/CD	14.90		❏	128	DJANGO REINHARDT - "GYPSY JAZZ" w/GUITAR	BK/CD	15.90
❏	63	TOM HARRELL	BK/CD	14.90		❏	129	A JAZZY CHRISTMAS	BK/CD	16.90
❏	64	"SALSA, LATIN, JAZZ"	BK/CD	14.90		❏	130	"PENNIES FROM HEAVEN"	BK/2CDs	19.95
❏	65	"FOUR & MORE" w/ORGAN	BK/2CDs	19.95		❏	131	"CRY ME A RIVER"	BK/CD	16.90
❏	66	BILLY STRAYHORN - "LUSH LIFE"	BK/CD	15.90		❏	132	"ON THE STREET WHERE YOU LIVE"	BK/CD	16.90
		All prices subject to change without notice. Visit www.jazzbooks.com for current pricing information.				❏	133	"DOWN BY THE RIVERSIDE" - DIXIELAND CLASSICS	BK/CD	16.90